This book belongs to.

MJ Cael

Date:

What Do You Like to Do...

Catholic Easy Reader
and Keepsake Journal

Nancy Nicholson

For Little Folks
www.forlittlefolks.com

Dedicated to Mary,

Virgin Mother of God the Son,

who treasured His childhood

in her heart

Copyright © 2010 Theresa A. Johnson

What Do You Like to Do... is under copyright. All rights reserved. No part of this book may be reproduced in any form by any means—electronic, mechanical, or graphic—without prior written permission. Thank you for honoring copyright law.

ISBN: 978-0-9883797-9-4

Printed by Sheridan Books, Inc.
Chelsea, Michigan   July 2014
Print code: 361331

For Little Folks
P.O. Box 571
Dresden, OH 43821
www.forlittlefolks.com

Distributed by
Catholic Heritage Curricula
P.O. Box 579090, Modesto, CA 95357
1-800-490-7713   www.chcweb.com

Contents

Introduction and Instructions, *page 1*

Spring, *page 3*

Summer, *page 47*

Fall, *page 75*

Winter, *page 103*

Sunday, *page 131*

Introduction and Instructions

The reading level in this book is suitable for the child who has completed *Little Stories for Little Folks,* Level 2. [For the child who is learning to read using a different reading program, *Little Stories for Little Folks: Catholic Phonics Readers* also offers further reading practice.]

Stories center around short vowel words in the beginning, then progress gently to include basic long vowel construction.

As the child reads what other children like to do in various seasons, he is invited to include his own stories and/or drawings or photos in the journal pages provided. [Each story's illustrations may also be colored, if desired.] These personal accounts not only give the child a special "ownership" of his book, but also create a treasured record of these precious years.

[To preserve the child's enthusiasm at this beginning writing level, it is best to allow him or her to write without correction.]

SPRING

1

Max likes to do tricks with his dog.

In the spring, Max likes to do tricks with his dog.

"This is Ruff. I got him as a pup. He is the best pet. You can tell him to do tricks," says Max.

"Sit, Ruff," says Max.

Ruff sits.

"Stand up on your back legs, Ruff!" Max tells his dog.

Ruff sits.

"Beg, Ruff, beg!" says Max.

Ruff sits.

"Bark, Ruff, bark!" says Max.

Ruff sits.

Max looks at Ruff.

"I think sitting is Ruff's best trick. Ruff, you are not a dog," says Max.

"You are a nut."

2

Tess likes to swing.

In the spring, Tess likes to swing.

She sings a happy song as she gets up on the swing.

Tess pumps her legs back and forth, back and forth.

The swing goes faster and faster. Up, up, up goes the swing.

Tess hangs on with both hands. She will not fall off.

Tess tips back on the swing and looks up at the sun.

She says, "Swings are happy things!"

And that is what Tess likes to do in the spring.

3

Rob likes to fish.

In the spring, Rob likes to fish with his Dad.

Rob and Dad sit on a big rock by the pond.

Rob's hook is in the water.

A big fish swims past.

The fish tugs on the hook.

Rob tugs back, hard.

He hooks the big fish!

Flip! Flop! The floppy fish lands on Rob's rock.

Oh, no! Will it slip back into the water?

Stop, fish!

Dad grabs a net. He sticks the net under the fish.

Dad helps Rob get the fish.

Rob is glad to fish with his dad.

And that is what Rob likes to do in the spring.

4

Liz likes to sip tea.

In the spring, Liz likes to sip tea with her doll and her cat, Fluff. She wants to have a tea party.

Liz will dress up for the tea party.

She puts on a big wig.

She puts on a floppy hat.

She puts a table cloth on her little table.

Then Liz sets the table with her best doll cups and dishes.

She fills her tea pot with tea.

Then she fills her cup to the top.

Liz sips the hot tea. Not a drop is spilled.

Liz tips the pot and puts a little bit of tea in the doll's cup.

Then the wig slips.

Liz will put a little bit of tea in Fluff's cup.

Oops! Too bad Liz can't see.

5

Tom likes to look for frogs.

In the spring, Tom likes to look for frogs.

He sees a fat frog sitting next to a big puddle.

There is just a little bit of water in the big puddle, but there is a lot of mud.

Tom wants to get the frog. With little steps, Tom gets almost up to the frog.

Then the frog sees Tom. With a hop and a splash, the frog jumps into the middle of the puddle.

The frog swims to a log. He hops on top of the log and looks at Tom.

Tom still wants to get that frog, but he does not want to get in the mud.

He gets a long, long stick. He wants to get the frog with the stick.

He has the stick in his hands. But the stick is too big for Tom.

Tom trips over the stick and slips on the mud.

Splash! Tom falls into the muddy puddle.

Tom sits in the mud and looks at the frog. He is not happy.

The frog looks back at Tom. He looks happy, sitting on his log. Do frogs grin?

6

Ben likes to see the baby animals.

In the spring, Ben likes to see all the little baby animals at Grandpa's. He likes to see the baby ducks and kids.

Last spring, Grandpa had a box in the back of his pick-up truck. The box had little baby ducks in it.

Grandpa dumped water in a tub. Then he took the baby ducks from the box. He put the little ducks in the tub of water.

The little ducks swam in the tub. They paddled back and forth in the water.

Then a little kid ran over to the tub. The frisky kid hopped and jumped. He stood up on his back legs and looked at the little ducks.

The frisky kid took a drink from the water in the ducks' tub.

Then a baby duck jumped up on the kid's back!

Ben likes Grandpa's funny animals.

And that's what Ben likes to do in the spring.

7

Alex likes to go to Easter Mass.

Easter comes in the spring. It is the wonderful day that Jesus rose from the dead!

In his bedroom, Alex is dressing to go to Easter Mass.

Alex wants to look his best for this holy day.

He puts on his best shirt. He buttons it all the way up. Then he clips on a black neck tie, just like Dad's.

Looking his best is a way that Alex can tell Jesus that he loves Him. Alex wants to look his best on the inside, too.

Before Holy Mass starts, he will put his fingers in the holy water font and bless himself, in the Name of the Father, and of the Son, and of the Holy Spirit.

Then he will sit and look at Jesus on the cross.

Alex says, "Dear Jesus, come to live inside me forever. Help me to be good always."

And Alex will be on time for Holy Mass. He doesn't want to miss anything on this wonderful Easter Day!

And that's what Alex likes to do in the spring.

What do you like to do in the spring?

Todd likes to help his dad cut wood.

In the spring, Todd likes to help his dad cut wood.

Todd lives up north. The winters are cold, and a wood stove keeps his home warm.

Todd's family must get wood in the spring and summer. If they wait too late to get wood, it will be winter again!

Todd's dad cuts the wood. Todd's job is to take the wood to the wood shed. He will put the wood in a

pile. Then his dad will stack the wood inside the shed.

Todd picks up the wood and stacks it in his wagon. He likes to pretend he is a horse and pull the wagon fast.

Trot, trot! Todd the Horse runs fast, pulling his wagon behind.

Gallop! Gallop! Todd the Horse runs faster and faster along the path to the wood shed.

Bump! Bump! The wagon hits a bump in the path. The wagon tips and the wood spills in the grass.

Todd is not a horse any more. He pretends that he is a strong man, picking up tall trees. It is fun to pretend and help Dad, too.

And that is what Todd likes to do in the spring.

Beth likes to plant flowers.

In the spring, Beth likes to plant pink and red and yellow snapdragons. Her mom says she likes the happy colors.

Beth puts snapdragon seeds in a pot. Then she pats dirt on top of the seeds.

Beth sets the pot in the sun, on the deck. She waters the seeds, asleep under the dirt.

Soon, little green plants pop up from the dirt. The snapdragon stems get taller and taller.

Beth has a happy plan. In the summer, the snapdragons will have little colored buds on the stems. Then the buds will open and bloom.

Beth will cut the tall stems with the colorful pink and red and yellow blooms.

She will put the snapdragons behind her back and take them to the living room.

Beth will ask her mom, "Can you tell what I have behind my back? Don't peek!"

She will put the colorful snapdragons in a glass of water and set them on the table just for Mom.

And that's what Beth likes to do in the spring—and summer!

10

Ned likes to play the drum.

It is a rainy spring day. Ned will play inside today. He can think of something to do. He will make something fun.

Ned wants to play the drum. That is a problem. Ned does not have a drum!

Ned thinks and thinks. He can make a drum. An oatmeal box is the same shape as a drum. He will ask Mom for an old oatmeal box.

"Mom," Ned asks, "please may I have an old oatmeal box? I want to make a drum."

"Yes, I have an oatmeal box," Mom says.

"There is a little bit of oatmeal left in it. Let me put the oatmeal in a can.

Then you will have an empty box for your drum."

Ned thanks his mom and takes the box to the table. He gets a sheet of red paper and colors lines on it. Then he glues the paper to the sides of the box. Ned prints his name on the side of the box. The box makes a fine looking drum.

Bam! Bam! Ned slaps his hands on top of the box.

"Come see my box drum, Mom!" says Ned.

"I don't need to see your box drum," smiles Mom. "I can hear it very well."

And that is what Ned likes to do on rainy spring days.

What do you like to do on rainy spring days?

In the spring, I like to

SUMMER

11
Sara and Livia like to have picnics.

In the summer, Sara and Livia like to have picnics in the yard.

They put a table cloth on the grass.

Then they put hot dogs and green salad and frosted cupcakes on the table cloth.

Sara and Livia will sit on the table cloth and have a feast.

Boom! Crash! Boom!

Thunder rumbles across the yard.

It is a thunder storm!

Rain begins to fall.

Sara and Livia jump up.

They grab the food and the table cloth and run as fast as they can.

They must get inside, away from the thunder storm!

Sadly, there will be no picnic today.

Wait!

Sara and Livia can still have a picnic!

They can put the table cloth on the floor.

Sara and Livia can sit on the table cloth and have a summer feast inside, safe from the storm.

12

Nick likes to collect rocks.

> * New sound: **ch**
>
> **ch**eeks   bea**ch**

Nick lives in Australia. In the summer, he likes to collect rocks, just like his dad. His dad told him where to find the best rocks on the beach.

Before he goes to the beach, Nick puts on a hat to keep the hot sunshine off his cheeks and nose, just like his dad.

He takes along a pail. He will put the stones that he finds into the pail and take them home.

Nick likes to wiggle the sand between his toes. He likes to run from the waves as they crash onto the sand. Sometimes the waves are faster than Nick and he gets splashed. Hunting for rocks is fun, but running from the waves is fun, too.

When the waves pull back, Nick looks for smooth stones that are left behind. The wet stones shine in the sun.

Nick picks up the best rocks and drops them in his pail. When he gets home, he will line the smooth rocks up by the back door.

His dad can see the shiny stones when he gets home from his job at the rock museum.*

And that's what Nick likes to do in the summer.

*Nick's dad is a *geologist*, a person who studies the earth and rocks.

13

Van likes to wait for his dad's boat.

Van's dad is a fisherman. He fishes on the sea all summer long. Van likes to wait on the dock until he can see his dad's boat coming into the bay. Today, the sun is sparkling on the water. It is hard to see across the bay with the sun shining on the water. Van waits, and thinks.

His dad spends weeks at sea, getting fish in his nets. He pulls the nets full of fish into the boat. Then he brings fish back to the cannery. There, the fish will

be put into cans and sold in stores for people to eat on Fridays!

Sometimes, Van thinks of the storms and big waves at sea. Then he remembers that St. Peter was a fisherman, too. Sometimes Jesus went fishing with St. Peter.

One time, during a storm, St. Peter was afraid that his boat was going to sink. Jesus made the storm stop so St. Peter was safe. Van is glad that Jesus is always with Dad on his fishing boat, too.

Van thinks and waits. Suddenly, he sees his dad's boat coming! He waves both arms back and forth, back and forth until his dad sees him.

Van is glad that his dad has come home. For Van, that is the best part of summer.

14

Jon likes to feed the geese.

Jon likes to feed the geese that come to the pond near his home.

This fall, he wants to feed lots of corn to the geese.

Dad told Jon that he can plant corn in the back yard. Dad will help him dig the dirt to make a garden. Then Jon can plant yellow corn for the geese in the wet, black dirt.

God makes the sun shine. The corn comes up, but weeds come up, too. Jon tugs and tugs to pull the weeds. Weeding makes his arms strong!

In the hot summer sun, the little corn plants get thirsty.

Jon fills a bucket to the top with water. The bucket is hard to pick up, but Jon is strong. He gives the thirsty plants a drink.

The corn gets taller and taller in the back yard garden.

The corn will be ripe in late summer. Then Jon will pick the corn and feed it to the geese at the pond.

And that is what Jon likes to do in the summer.

What do you like to do in the summer?

15

Josh likes to visit his uncle.

In the summer, Josh likes to visit Uncle Warren at his log cabin in the forest.

The cabin is far up in the hills. Not very many people live near Uncle Warren's cabin. But there are many animals in the forest. There is a creek with silvery fish and mossy rocks. Josh likes to wade in the creek on hot days.

One day, Uncle Warren took Josh into the forest.

Uncle Warren had two sacks, one for Josh, and one for himself.

Uncle Warren and Josh picked up fat, sticky pine cones under the pine trees. They put the pine cones in the sacks and took them back to the cabin.

Uncle Warren and Aunt Moe use the pine cones to start a fire in the wood stove. The pine cones snap and crackle and help make a hot fire. Aunt Moe makes blueberry pancakes on the hot stove. Josh is glad that he helped get pine cones. He likes blueberry pancakes!

The last day of Josh's visit, Aunt Moe took him for a walk by the bubbling creek. She pointed to deer tracks by the creek and then put her finger to her lips. She pointed into the woods. There, Josh saw a mama deer and her new baby, hiding in the woods!

And that is what Josh likes to do in the summer.

What do you like to do in the summer?

In the summer, I like to

74

FALL

16

Ellen likes to visit an old park.

Ellen lives near London. In the fall, she likes to visit an old, old park. It is fun to skip under the tall trees that line the sidewalks.

Ellen looks up at the old, old trees. She thinks of brave saints that went to prison for their Faith. Maybe they went past some of these trees on the way to prison. She asks God to make her brave like the saints.

In the fall, the park looks different than it did in the summer. The trees were green in the summer. In the fall, they turn shades of red and yellow. It is as if God painted the trees in fall colors.

A breeze rustles in the trees. Leaves fall onto the walk. They crunch under Ellen's feet as she skips along the sidewalk.

Ellen sees piles and piles of pretty leaves that cover the grass and sidewalks. She gathers red leaves and green leaves and yellow leaves in her arms.

She takes the leaves home and presses them between the pages of a book. That way, the leaves will last a long time.

The leaves remind her of her happy fall walk in the park of saints.

And that's what Ellen likes to do in the fall.

What do you like to do in the fall?

17

Teesha Maree likes to play with her pet rabbit.

In the fall, Teesha Maree likes to play with her pet rabbit, Bugs.

Bugs lives in a cage, and it is Teesha's job to keep the cage clean. Teesha sets Bugs on the grass and pulls dirty hay from the cage.

She fills his water bottle with clean, fresh water. She hangs the water bottle upside down on the side of the cage so Bugs can lick the end and get a drink.

Then Teesha puts new hay in the corner of the cage. Bugs can eat the hay, and sleep in the hay.

Teesha takes good care of her pet.

Teesha is finished cleaning the cage. She sits on the grass in the shade. Bugs hops over to sit in her lap. Teesha gives him a long blade of grass to nibble and pets his soft fur.

His long ears flick back and forth as he nibbles the grass. The blade of grass gets shorter and shorter as Bugs chews and chews. Then he starts to nibble Teesha's fingers.

"Stop, Bugs! My fingers are not grass! You are a funny bunny," says Teesha.

And that is what Teesha Maree likes to do in the fall.

18

Maddy and J.J. like to play indoor baseball.

In the fall, Maddy and J.J. like to play indoor baseball.

They ask Mama for some old newspapers and cardboard tubes. Maddy and J.J. make piles and piles of paper balls from the newspaper pages. Then they use the cardboard tubes to bat the balls across the living room.

It is O.K. to bat the paper balls in the living room.

They are soft and will not hurt the walls or chairs or sofa.

Soon, the living room floor is covered with newspaper balls. Mom says, "Time to clean up this mess!"

Mom sets a box in the middle of the living room. She brings a long bit of string into the living room and lays it in a line across the floor.

"Time for a new game!" Mom says. "Stand behind this line. Toss the paper balls into the box. The person that gets the most paper balls in the box is the winner."

Mom likes this game best, for the living room is clean again in no time.

And that is what Maddy and J.J. and Mom like to do in the fall.

19

Pete likes frosty fall days.

> * New word: **ice**

In the fall, Pete can hardly wait for the first frosty day.

On the first freezing day, Pete pulls on his mittens and boots, zips up his jacket and runs into the yard to look for frozen puddles.

There is frost on the grass and frost on the fallen leaves. And in one corner of the yard is a big frozen puddle. The water has frozen into **ice**.*

Pete runs to the puddle and slides back and forth on the **ice**. Then he slips and falls on his bottom! Pete even likes the falling part of sliding on frozen puddles.

Then Pete starts to stomp on the **ice**. Stomp, stomp! Crack! Crack! Pete's boots crack the **ice**.

Pete picks up chunks of **ice**. He holds them up to the sun and looks into the **ice**. The **ice** is like a chunk of clear glass. Pete can still see the sun in the **ice**.

The **ice** begins to melt, and Pete's mittens get wet. He takes them off and holds the cold **ice** in his bare hands.

Brrrrr! It is time to go inside.

And that is what Pete likes to do on frosty fall days.

Alma and Manuel like to dress up for All Saints' Day.

In the fall, Alma and Manuel like to dress up for All Saints' Day. They are going to a costume party at the parish hall. Even the bishop is going to come!

"Dad will drive you to the parish hall at five o'clock this Friday," Mama says. "We still have lots of time to make simple costumes if you pick a saint soon."

Alma says, "I will dress up like Our Lady. I can make a blue mantle and glue some stars on it."

Manuel says, "I will be St. Juan Diego. I can make a tan cape to wear, if Alma will help me."

All of a sudden, Alma thinks of a surprise.

"Maybe Mama will let us pick the last roses from our garden!"

"Mama, please may we pick the last roses from the garden?" asks Alma. "At the party, I will give them to Manuel.

"We will make a big surprise. Manuel can hide the roses in his cape, just like St. Juan Diego.

"Then he can drop the roses on the floor at the bishop's feet!"

And that's what Alma and Manuel like to do in the fall.

What do you like to do in the fall?

In the fall, I like to

WINTER

21
Evie likes to ice skate.

In the winter, Evie likes to ice skate. Evie lives in Canada, near a lake.

She waits to skate until the lake ice has frozen hard.

She never, never, never goes to the lake until her Dad says it has frozen hard.

When it freezes hard, it is safe to step and slide and skate on the ice.

Evie wants to do what Dad tells her.

She wants to be safe. Then she can have fun ice skating.

"It is so cold today!" Dad tells Evie. "The lake has frozen hard. You can go skating today."

Evie claps her hands and runs to get her ice skates. She puts on her coat and hat and mittens.

Evie waits until she gets to the lake to put on her skates.

She has a happy time skating back and forth on the frozen lake.

That's what Evie likes to do in the winter.

What do you like to do in the winter?

22

Dan waits for a happy feast day.

In the winter, Dan and his family wait for a happy feast day that is coming soon.

Dan and his family cut a pine tree in the forest near their home. They take the pine tree home and put it in the middle of the living room.

Dan's mother puts a clean sheet under the tree. Some green needles fall on the clean sheet. Dan likes the smell of the pine needles.

Dan opens a box with some red and blue glass balls inside. He is careful with the glass balls. He hangs the shining balls on the tree.

Dan's dad puts a shiny silver star at the top of the pine. The star reminds Dan of a star that shone long ago, in a land far away. That star shone over the crib of the Son of God.

Waiting for this happy feast day is what Dan likes to do best in winter.

Can you tell what feast day Dan and his family are waiting for?

23

Lupe likes to help her mom bake a cake.

In the winter, Lupe likes to help her mom bake a cake for Three Kings' Day.

Sometimes the Three Kings are called Wise Men. Lupe remembers that the Wise Men came from far away to see Baby Jesus, the Infant King. The Wise Men remind us that Jesus came to save all people, near and far.

Lupe helps her mom. She beats eggs and milk in

a big pan. Soon the cake will go into the hot stove.

When the cake has baked, Lupe will help her mom frost the cake. The cake will have golden yellow frosting, to remind them of the gold the Wise Men gave to Baby Jesus.

After the cake is all frosted, it will sit in the middle of the table, on top of a clean table cloth.

[And sometimes, Lupe gets to lick the frosting spoon. Do you like to lick the frosting spoon?]

Lupe will put silverware and plates and napkins on the table. Then the family will have a Three Kings' Party!

Baking a cake for Three Kings' Day is what Lupe likes to do in the winter.

What do you like to do in the winter?

24

Carlos likes to see the roadrunner birds.

Carlos lives in the desert. In the spring, Carlos likes to see the desert roadrunner birds build a stick nest in the prickly cactus in his yard.

All summer long, Carlos gets to see the baby roadrunners hopping after insects to eat. The animals of the desert don't mind the summer heat, so Carlos sometimes sees snakes and lizards, too.

Even in the winter, it is warm in the desert so the animals still come and go. Sometimes big snakes

come into Carlos' yard, and even onto the deck! But roadrunners like to eat snakes. Carlos' mom says roadrunners are her favorite bird. Every winter, she makes little meatballs for the roadrunners to eat. She gives the meatballs to Carlos to put on the deck. Then the roadrunners come up on the deck for their dinner!

One roadrunner is very brave. Carlos has named this brave bird "BeepBeep." If he is hungry, BeepBeep walks across the deck and up to the door. Then BeepBeep pecks on the door! Carlos opens the door and gives the smart bird a meatball.

And that is what Carlos likes to do in the winter.

What do you like to do in the winter?

25

Dominic and Kim like to fingerpaint.

On cold winter days, Dominic and his baby sister Kim like to fingerpaint in the bath tub.

"Mom, please may we play with the fingerpaints?" Dominic asks.

"Ya!" says Kim.

"Hmmm. Let me read the fingerpaint jar first," says Mom. "O.K., it says this paint is safe even for a baby.

"You can put on old T-shirts and shorts, and then you can fingerpaint in the bath tub."

Dominic paints a yellow sun on the side of the tub.

Kim paints her nose blue.

Dominic paints a red horse next to the yellow sun.

Kim paints her hair blue.

Dominic paints a green tree next to the horse.

Kim paints her lips blue.

Mom peeks into the bathroom and says, "Eek! What are you doing?"

"I'm painting the tub," says Dominic.

"I eating poo-ding," says Kim.

And that's what Dominic and Kim like to do in the winter.

What do you like to do in the winter?

In the winter, I like to

Sunday

26

Luke likes the Lord's Day best of all.

On the Lord's Day, this is what Luke likes to do.

Luke starts his day with the best part of the day, and the most important part of the week. He goes to Holy Mass with his dad and mom and sisters and brothers!

After Holy Mass, Luke and his six sisters and brothers go to Grandma and Grandpa's house for dinner.

Everybody helps in some way. Luke's dad makes an apple salad to take along, and his mom makes sweet rolls. Luke and his sisters and brothers take turns setting the table before dinner, and washing dishes after.

But Luke's favorite part of the visit isn't the dinner. His favorite part of the visit is hearing Grandpa tell stories about when Luke's dad was a little boy.

Luke's favorite story is about when his dad was little and wanted to be a

logger, so he chopped down Grandma's rose bush with an ax. Grandma was so upset that Dad had to stay in his room for the rest of the week!

When everyone is seated at the dinner table, Grandpa says the blessing. Then each person at the table says one thing he is thankful for. For Luke, it is always the same thing. He thanks God for the wonderful blessing of his big family.

What do you like to do on the Lord's Day?

On the Lord's
Day, I like to

Teach your child to read with...
Little Stories for Little Folks

Catholic Phonics Readers

Distributed by

Catholic Heritage Curricula

P.O. Box 579090, Modesto, California 95357

To request a free catalog, call toll-free: 1-800-490-7713
Or visit online: *www.chcweb.com*

If your child enjoyed and benefited from this book, perhaps you would also enjoy some of CHC's other homeschooling materials, whether for extra practice outside of school, homeschooling, or character development.

Other titles by Nancy Nicholson:
- *I Can Find Letter Sounds*
- *I Can Find Numbers and Shapes*
- *Little Folks' Letter Practice*
- *Little Folks' Number Practice*
- *Little Stories for Little Folks: Catholic Phonics Readers*
- *What Can You Do… Easy Reader & Keepsake Journal*
- *Bigger Stories for Little Folks*
- *Devotional Stories for Little Folks*
- *Devotional Stories for Little Folks, Too*
- *My Catholic Speller Series*
- *Language of God Series*
- *Catholic Heritage Handwriting Series*
- *Behold and See 1 & 2 Science*
- *High School of Your Dreams*